Dear Jim

Happy 50ths!

THINGS TO DO NOW THAT YOU'RE 50

Lots of love from,
George, Karen
Kristen, Matt
and Brianna

2006

# things to do now

ROBERT ALLEN    Illustrations by Robyn Neild

*that you're* 50

MQP

# contents

1 at home and abroad...6

2 career and lifestyle...38

3 activities and hobbies...72

4 nurturing the outer you...104

5 ambitions and goals...132

6 friends and family...162

7 love and romance...192

8 exploring the inner you...222

# at home and abroad

*Visit Eastern Europe quickly before it becomes just the same as everywhere else.*

Climb to the top of La Sagrada Familia cathedral in Barcelona, Spain. Literally breathtaking!

*Make sure you go on safari in Africa at least once in your life.*

*Go to see the Bayeux Tapestry in France. But be sure to go in the off-peak season. In the tourist season the line is so long it'd be quicker to knit one of your own.*

*At least once in your life go to see the
aurora borealis (northern lights).*

A visit to the Dali Museum in Figueres
(northeastern Spain) is like being dropped into
the middle of one of his paintings. You can also
visit his house in Port Lligat. But if you can't get
there, visit the Dali Museum in St. Petersburg,
Florida, and see its impressive collection.

*Remember all those westerns you
saw as a kid? Go and take a look
at Monument Valley in Utah.
It will bring it all to life for you.*

**Take the one you love for a relaxing trip
down Germany's Romantische Strasse.**

Visit the Tower of London and see where all those royals got the chop. It's informative and fun— in a gruesome sort of way.

*Climb Mount Fuji. You can stay overnight in one of the huts near the crater and climb down the next day.*

Go for a walk on the Great Wall of China. It's the only man-made object visible from space so remember to wave to all those aliens!

*Visit base camp at Mount Everest. You don't have to climb the mountain but you should at least have a close-up look at it.*

Investigate the history of your community. Find out at least one interesting thing that no one has discovered before.

*Go whitewater rafting and experience the adrenaline rush of a lifetime.*

Make a point of visiting Uluru (Ayers Rock) in Australia. But don't take a piece home with you—they say the rock brings bad luck to those who steal bits.

Go to Malibu and learn to surf, or for something even more adventurous, try sand surfing in the magnificent sand dunes of Rio Grande do Norte in Brazil.

*Go scuba diving in some of the world's most spectacular locations: try the Great Barrier Reef, the Red Sea, or the Barrier Reef off Belize.*

*Hire an off-road vehicle and take the drive of a lifetime across the roughest, toughest country you can find.*

*Have a go at teaching English abroad. It would pay for a lengthy vacation in one of your favorite far-flung places.*

*Make a list of all the places you want to visit and try to cross off at least one of them each year.*

How well do you know your own country? Make a list of all the parts you've never visited and work your way through them.

Try to arrange a trip to Antarctica. It's not easy to get to, but it is the last major wilderness in the world so it would be well worth the effort.

*Take part in a conservation project either at home or abroad. Save one of the world's wild places and enjoy yourself at the same time.*

Take a trip on a minisubmarine. This will be expensive but how many people can boast that they've seen the bottom of the ocean?

Visit the Middle East and "do" a Lawrence of Arabia: travel by camel across a sea of sand dunes.

Travel by elephant through the Golden Triangle (the hill regions of Thailand, Burma, and Laos). It's a little dangerous but that is part of the charm—and you can bet that few of your friends will have done it.

Work your passage around the world on a cruise liner or, if you're really tough, on a merchant ship.

*Hire quad bikes and head
for the open countryside.
It doesn't matter too much
where you go, the thrill comes
from bouncing around on one
of those tough little bikes.*

*Why not spend a vacation pony-trekking in the wild?*

Next time you're in a big city,
just get on the first bus you see
and let it take you to an unknown
destination. You're bound to get
a surprise of some sort and it just
might be a really good one.

*Make sure that you cross the
Equator by boat at least once.*

*Go shopping by night in Barcelona's La Rambla district—a weird, wonderful experience that you won't forget.*

*When in Southeast Asia, make a point of buying and eating a durian fruit. The smell is disgusting but just hold your nose and eat some——the flavor is well worth the effort.*

Take a vacation picking grapes for a winery. You get exercise and sunshine, and they let you drink the wine after work.

Quick, visit St. Petersburg, Russia before they change the name again! While there make sure you drop in at the Hermitage museum.

*Take a trip to Moscow. If you're tough enough, go in winter and relive all those* Dr. Zhivago *moments.*

Take the tour of London's Buckingham Palace. They also let you see the gardens and watch the changing of the guard. It's a unique experience.

*If you haven't taken the tour of the Statue of Liberty, you've really missed out. Give it a try!*

*A gondola trip in Venice is expensive and may be a bit of a cliché, but it's a magical experience.*

Take a punt (a flat-bottomed boat) out on the river in the university cities of Cambridge or Oxford. Don't worry about falling in as the water is shallow—mostly!

Visit Jerusalem, the center of three major faiths. It is also the only place on Earth where the cab drivers will argue with you about archaeology.

*Why not take a trip to see a tropical rain forest? If things don't improve on the ecology front, ours may be the last generation that can still make this journey.*

*Climb the Mayan pyramids of Mexico (you don't have to complete all of them). It's a challenging but rewarding experience. These pyramids are some of the most mysterious objects on Earth.*

*Travel the klongs (canals) of Bangkok in a long-tail boat. It's powered by a small car engine and reaches impressive speeds.*

Have you ever tried a home swap? You can meet other families via the Internet and arrange a vacation in which you swap homes. It saves on hotel bills and lets you see how other people live.

*Are you tired of the usual Christmas holidays? You could visit Lapland and meet Santa Claus in person.*

At Christmas, go and listen to the choir of King's College Chapel in Cambridge, England. You have to get in line really early in the morning, but there is a great camaraderie among visitors from all over the world.

*Take a walk among the giant trees in Sequoia National Park. These are some of the oldest living things on earth.*

Resistance is useless—you simply must see Disney World or one of its offshoots. We're all just kids at heart.

*You simply can't die until you've seen Machu Picchu——the lost city of the Incas. It's on the eastern side of the Andes in Peru.*

*Angkor Wat in Cambodia has spectacular architecture, history, and breathtaking landscape all in one place.*

If you ever feel depressed about the state of the world, go to the site of the former Berlin Wall and remind yourself that good stuff happens too.

*This one will do some serious harm to your bank balance, but you really must see the Galápagos Islands, Ecuador. They have the most spectacular wildlife.*

*If you're in London, pick a sunny day (yes, they do exist!) to ride on the London Eye ferris wheel. You'll get a wonderful view of the whole city.*

*Climb the Eiffel Tower and see Paris from above.*

If you visit Holyrood Palace in Edinburgh, look for the room where Queen Mary's favorite, David Rizzio, was brutally murdered. It's said the bloodstains cannot be removed from the floor.

Take a trip on the Orient Express.

*Take a year off work and spend it traveling around the world.*

*Take a walk up an active volcano. Make sure it isn't erupting at the time, though.*

Pay a visit to Kronborg Castle, Elsinore, Denmark, which is famed as the setting for Shakespeare's *Hamlet*.

*Travel to the Netherlands in spring just in time for the tulips.*

Visit the geyser called Old Faithful (there are actually two—one in Yellowstone National Park and another in California).

Go to Jordan and visit Petra, the
"rose red city half as old as time."

*The Grand Canyon is a must.*
*You will never see anything so*
*spectacular again.*

Visit the Niagara Falls.
People used to try going over
the falls in a barrel, but this
is not recommended.

*If you really hate snakes, don't ever go to Bangkok's*
*Pasteur Institute where they have hundreds of live ones*
*on display. But if you think snakes are cool, this is one*
*place you just have to visit.*

# *Visit the famous Terracotta Army at Xi'An in China.*

Go to Singapore, register at the famous Raffles Hotel, and order a Singapore Sling at the bar.

*Visit Tintagel in Cornwall, England. It is said to be the site of King Arthur's castle.*

While in Cornwall, take a trip to Land's End. It is the southwesterly tip of the country and is famous for its wild coast and shipwrecks.

Everyone should see Rome,
the hub of Western civilization.

In Rouen, France, you can visit the spot where
Joan of Arc was burned at the stake by the English.

Take a trip to the Bermuda Triangle,
which is situated between Bermuda,
Puerto Rico, and Miami, Florida,
and is said to be the site of many
mysterious disappearances.

At Mount Rushmore you not only get to
see the famous US presidents but also
the scene of the denouement of
Hitchcock's thriller North by
Northwest starring Cary Grant.

*In Paris you can climb to the top of Notre Dame and see the view. While you're there, do your Charles Laughton impression: "The bells! The bells!"*

*Take your partner to the Taj Mahal and enjoy India's most romantic spot.*

When in India you must learn to chew betel nut. It is a bit of an acquired taste (and turns your saliva bright red) but if you persist, you'll get to like it.

Want to try something just a bit different? The Capuchins' catacombs in Palermo, Italy, have thousands of corpses lined on the walls like paintings. A visit would make an unusual day out.

On the last Wednesday of August, the village of Bunol, Spain, stages a tomato war. For two hours the whole town goes crazy as people pelt each other with ripe tomatoes. Why not join in?

Gansbaai in S. Africa is called the world capital of the Great White Shark. Go there and you can be taken on trip to photograph these superb creatures in the wild—if you dare!

*If you want to enjoy the sun in ideal surroundings, why not fly down to Rio de Janeiro and relax in style on Copacabana Beach?*

*Here's an unusual treat for archaeology buffs. At Newgrange in Ireland you can see the largest neolithic burial chamber in Europe. It is so old that it even predates Egypt's pyramids.*

*Prague, capital of the Czech Republic, is the coolest city in Europe these days, so go and check it out.*

*Have you seen whales in the wild? You can do this in Hawaii or in many parts of Europe.*

In Bangkok, you can watch Thai kick boxing. They'll even let you take on one of their fighters. Be warned—they may be small but they pack one heck of a punch!

Visit the American cemetery near Cambridge, England. It's a memorial to the aircrew who lost their lives in the Second World War.

When in Texas, how about a trip to San Antonio to see the site of the famous Battle of the Alamo? You've seen it often enough in the movies—now see the real thing.

There are many reasons to visit Amsterdam, not least of which is that you can visit Anne Frank's house.

*Go and visit the Leaning Tower of Pisa in Italy. You can take that old favorite trick photo where you appear to be holding the tower up.*

*Go to see the running of the bulls in Pamplona. You can join in if you think you're fast enough.*

Become a stargazer. Once you get hooked, you will enjoy it for life. Just think, you can travel unimaginable distances while sitting at home.

*Take a journey through Florida's Everglades. Enjoy the unique environment (but mind the alligators).*

*If you love the history of the Wild West, take a trip to Montana and see the site of the Battle of the Little Bighorn, where Custer made his last stand.*

*Have you ever watched the traditional Scottish Highland games? You don't even need to go to Scotland to see them because they are regularly held in many parts of the world, especially the US and Canada.*

Play a game of jai alai, where you throw the ball using a long basket worn like a glove. You can play it in many parts of the US, or go to the Basque country where the game was born.

Go to the Normandy beaches in France and see exactly where the Allies landed on D-Day.

Golfers, how about playing a round at the home of golf—The Royal and Ancient Golf Club at St. Andrews, Scotland?

*Take a trip you'll never forget. Hong Kong's Tiger Balm Gardens are wild and wacky, and you'll kick yourself if you miss them.*

*A trip to Beijing, China, is well worth the long journey. In the post-Mao era, the place is really geared up for visitors.*

Go to Wales to visit Llanfairpwllgwyngyllgogerychwyrndrobwllllantysiliogogogoch. The locals will even teach you how to pronounce it.

If you'd like to do something really unusual, you could join the search for the Holy Grail. The cup Jesus used at the Last Supper is rumored to be still in existence and has miraculous properties. Could you be the one to find it?

While walking in the Alps, you can rest your tired feet in a Kneip bath. Invented by Dr. Kneip, the bath consists of a pool of freezing cold water with a base of stones. If it sounds painful, it is—but you feel wonderful after you get out.

*Make a point of seeing a Titan Arum. The plant produces a huge flower only once in many years and you have to be quick to catch it. But beware—it stinks!*

If you've not yet seen a total solar eclipse, you really should. But you may have to travel a long way. Check the Internet for the date of the next one.

Getting married? Las Vegas has much to offer. For example, you can tie the knot in a helicopter while flying over the Las Vegas Strip.

Have you ever felt like owning a racing pigeon? No? Well, maybe you should. The way they find their way home, no matter how far away they are released, is truly remarkable.

Each year, try to take your vacation somewhere you have never been before. You'll make some fascinating discoveries.

Every year in Portimão, Portugal, they hold a sardine festival. If you like parties, music, dancing, and, above all, eating grilled sardines, this could be the place for you.

*If the Wild West is your thing, go to northwestern Wyoming, where you'll find the Buffalo Bill Historical Center. It has all you want to know about the life and times of a remarkable character in American history.*

Make your own list of the Seven Wonders of the World, putting down all the places you've always wanted to visit and never got around to doing. Aim to visit all of them before you die.

Go and see a rodeo. You can find them all over the US and Canada; search on the Internet to find one close to you.

Go fishing for piranha. You can eat them, but most people have them stuffed as a souvenir. But mind your fingers!

*On January 25, you can hold a Burns Night supper in memory of Scots poet Robert Burns. Eat haggis, recite the traditional "Ode to a Haggis," drink single malt whisky, and enjoy the company of friends.*

How about searching for Nessie? Scotland's Loch Ness is supposedly home to a huge monster and many people swear that they've caught a glimpse of it. Could you be the one to provide irrefutable evidence?

*How about a double treat? In the fall, monarch butterflies leave the US and Canada to fly to Mexico just in time for the Mexican version of Halloween, called Los Dias de Los Muertos. You could see both in one trip.*

career
and lifestyle

*Think of the job you always wanted and go for it. Don't be satisfied with the safe second-best option.*

Train yourself to get up a bit earlier. The early morning, before the rush begins, is the best part of the day.

Make sure that your career teaches you something new at least once a month. If you're not learning from what you do, you may be in the wrong job.

*Make a master plan for your career and set time limits for each phase. The journey is long and you need a good map.*

Learn to recognize a big opportunity when you see it. You may only get the chance once and it would be too bad if you missed it.

*Take at least one big risk in your career. If you don't, you'll always wonder "What if..." and have regrets.*

*Work for a large company at least once. Never be satisfied with being a big fish in a little pond.*

Try working overseas at least once. Mix with the locals and get a new perspective on life.

*Have a plan for personal development and stick to it. Make regular improvements to yourself.*

*Always learn from life and continue to grow mentally and spiritually no matter how old you get.*

*Learn that happiness is something that you can make but never buy.*

Have at least one activity outside work that you are passionate about.

However high you rise up the corporate ladder, always make time for your family and friends  That way they'll still be around when the job is gone.

Make a point of remembering the ideals you had when you were young. Don't let age and experience make you cynical.

*Always be your own fiercest critic. Never let yourself get away with a shoddy job.*

*Make a point of talking to people who know more than you. Listen to what they have to say.*

*Make a speech to a large audience. Don't be intimidated by numbers, pick out one person at a time in the crowd and address your remarks to them.*

Use some of your spare time to study for extra qualifications that will help your career to progress.

*Pay into a pension plan so that you can enjoy your later years.*

Plant your own vegetable garden. There is no taste like that of your own freshly grown produce.

*Keep a diary in which to jot down good ideas as they come to you. Right now might not be the best time to follow them up, but one day you'll look at them and find just the bit of inspiration you need.*

What's the point of working hard unless you have time to enjoy it? Get your work/life balance right now so that you have no regrets later on.

*Be ambitious. No one ever won by planning how to come second.*

Re-evaluate your life. Write down all the good stuff and everything you dislike. Now you can plan ways to make the first list longer and the second shorter.

*Take time to study a little psychology. Learning what makes people tick will help you at home and at work.*

# When you see people you admire, learn how to emulate them.

*Just because you're getting older, it doesn't mean you should no longer celebrate your birthday. Make sure you make a big deal of your birthday every year from now on.*

*Laugh a lot. Make sure all your wrinkles are smile lines.*

*Give—make it a habit to be generous not just with money, but with your time and your energy.*

*Learn to manage your time. It can be hard to get everything done but if you make a schedule and stick to it, your life will run more smoothly.*

Learn to manage your money. "Money coming in" must be more than "money going out" or you're in trouble. It seems obvious, but many people never understand this.

Learn from other people's mistakes.

*Throw out all the junk that clutters up your home and office. It's a good idea to make a fresh start from time to time.*

Now throw out all the junk in your mind. Think of all the old grudges and resentments, regrets, and failed dreams. Make a list and then burn it and notice how much lighter you feel.

Try to have a good idea each day and a really good idea a few times every year. With luck, at least once in a lifetime you'll have a stroke of genius.

*At work, why not try to give the youngsters a leg up instead of putting them down? At your age you can afford to be generous.*

*At fifty, you should give a little thought to your retirement. If you plan it well in advance and deal with the issues now, it won't take you by surprise later on.*

Take a break from work each day and do some exercise. Most of us don't do enough and many do none at all. You'll feel fitter and more alert.

*Always keep one eye on your next job. Don't let familiarity make you get bogged down.*

Have you ever wanted to strike out on your own? Write a business plan and see whether you have an idea that will work.

In work you must always go the extra mile. Never be satisfied with doing just enough to keep out of trouble.

*Be a fortune-teller! Anticipate future trends in your business and be ready to benefit from them.*

*Work on your people skills. Your ability to handle people will contribute to about 90 percent of your success in life.*

# Don't ignore criticism, no matter how much it hurts— learn from it.

# Make a point of recognizing your strengths and playing to them.

*Be honest enough to recognize your weaknesses and work on eliminating them.*

 *Have you ever heard the saying, "It's not what you know but who you know that counts"? It's true. Get out there and meet people.*

*By your age you are probably in quite a senior position. Don't dwell on your past successes but always try to do something new.*

When dealing with co-workers, think how you look from their point of view. How would you feel if someone behaved the same way to you?

*Promise more than you can deliver and people will cease to trust you. Deliver more than you promise and they will be impressed.*

*Don't consider it acceptable to tell lies in business simply because the business world is tough—you'll get found out and your reputation will be as full of holes as Swiss cheese.*

Learn to be a good team player.
These days, everyone wants team players.

*Always show enthusiasm.
Nothing is more attractive and people
will constantly be drawn to you.*

*Make a point of giving people your
full attention. It is guaranteed to
make a good impression.*

Make all the days
of your life count.
This is the real thing,
not a trial run.

*When you're middle-aged, it's easy to get stuck in a rut,
so make sure you keep growing mentally and spiritually.*

*Be adventurous! It helps to keep life interesting for you and those around you.*

Occasionally, you should scare yourself. Do something that you never thought you'd dare to do.

*Now that you're grown up, never assume that Plan A will always work. Sometimes you'll be glad that you had Plan B all thought out.*

*However much you are tempted to do everything for your kids, let them do as much as possible for themselves.*

Don't waste time worrying about disasters that haven't happened yet. Remember the overblown fracas at the turn of the millennium when everyone thought the world was going to grind to a halt because of the so-called Millennium Bug?

*Recognize that sometimes you are wrong. When that happens, give in with good grace.*

*Remember that it's OK to screw up sometimes. How else do you expect to learn?*

In business, always get the small stuff right. It's no good being a genius if you don't deliver the goods on time.

*Unless you learn to talk with passion about your own ideas, how do you expect to sell them to anyone else?*

*If you don't believe in yourself by now, you probably never will—so work on it immediately.*

Make a point of having integrity. People may not say much but they will notice and think well of you.

Keep busy all the time. Never say, "I don't have time" because busy people always have time.

*Make a point of looking at the big picture now and then. That way your everyday worries will shrink.*

*Always simplify! Any idiot can make things complicated but it takes real brains to keep it simple.*

When you work don't try to do everything at once. Break your tasks into chunks and give each one your undivided attention. You'll be much more efficient that way.

Make a point once each year (maybe on New Year's Day) of reviewing your career and your life completely and honestly. Have you done all that you wanted? Have you achieved what you planned to achieve? What should you do in the coming year?

*Don't follow the money—follow your passions. If you are passionate enough about something, you will always succeed.*

*In business, when you talk to people you may sometimes stretch the truth a little. But never tell anything less than the naked truth to yourself.*

Say what you mean and mean what you say. This is old advice—so how come so many people never follow it?

*By the time you reach fifty, most of your life choices will have been made. But if you want, you still have time to make changes. Have the courage to make at least one really important change.*

Now that you are fifty, you will have experienced a lot. Give advice freely when asked for it, but if you're not asked, keep your big mouth shut!

*Learn to trust your subconscious. It works for you all the time, even when you are fast asleep. So when a thought pops into your consciousness take note. It didn't get there by accident.*

*Cultivate patience because it is part of the wisdom that comes with age.*

When about to take action, ask yourself, "Who will benefit?" and then "Will anyone be harmed?" Don't proceed unless you are happy with your answers.

*At fifty, people will look to you for leadership and answers. This is a great responsibility— be aware of it at all times.*

*If you are someone whose desk always looks like a junkyard, you should take time to tidy it. You'll be amazed how much better you can think without clutter to distract you.*

Arrange a job swap. For a short while, swap places with someone who does a similar job in another country. This will provide you both with interesting insights and new ideas.

*Learn to relax without feeling guilty. While you're relaxing, your mind is still working.*

*If your employer doesn't do regular appraisals, try to persuade them to. Unless you know what they think of you, how can you ever improve?*

Get to work early at least one day a week and you'll amaze yourself with how much more you get done when your mind is fresh and you're not distracted.

*No one teaches kids how to concentrate even though it's a vital skill. If you have a butterfly mind, make the effort to learn concentration and see how your efficiency improves.*

Always eat lunch! People who think lunch is for wimps are wrong. You'll work with extra vigor after a short break.

*Think of what you would want written on your headstone and try to live your life accordingly.*

*Rearrange your office and home on feng shui principles. You'll find not only that your serenity improves, but also that your energy levels increase.*

When you write office e-mails, make a point of considering how they will sound to the recipient. E-mails can often sound rude when you think you are just being businesslike.

*In business it is important to be aware of the possibility that you may be wrong. Consider contrary views carefully.*

Don't ignore stress—it won't just go away. Always find ways to relax and lessen your stress levels.

*As you grow older, try hard to grow wiser. This doesn't happen as a matter of course; you need to work at it.*

Learn to let the buck stop with you and do something about it.

*Make a point of never engaging in office politics and people will turn to you as someone they can trust.*

*When things go wrong at work, make sure you are the first to find a way to clear them up and the last to assign blame.*

*Before you get any older, do something about training your memory. Forgetfulness is not inevitable, but you have to work at preventing it.*

Now that you're fifty, you'll know that your time is not endless. Decide to make the best possible use of whatever time you have.

*If a retirement of pottering in the garden doesn't thrill you, why not plan a new business venture? Some people get huge enjoyment from a late career change.*

When you write an angry letter, make it a real ripsnorter. Then throw it out and write a more moderate one.

*Take nothing at face value. At your age you can appreciate subtleties and nuances that you would once have missed.*

Train yourself not to confuse activity with achievement. You can get away with doing less if what you do is always exactly the right thing.

*Business involves a lot of pointless communication. Before you write a letter, decide whether what you have to say is worth killing a tree.*

*Teach yourself to divide the time available by the amount of work to be done. It sounds simple, but many never get the hang of it.*

*Think—if you vanished tomorrow,
what would you be missed for most?
Those are the important things.
The rest is just incidental.*

Study ways to look after the
planet. People will want to use
it after you've finished with it.

*Always keep all the letters, e-mails,
and notes that prove conclusively
that it wasn't your fault!*

If you take days off sick because you can't
stand your job, ask yourself whether it is
you or the job that is really sick.

*Take all the training courses the company offers you. You can never learn too much.*

*Learn to work and not worry. Worrying never got anything done.*

Ask yourself from time to time, "Why does this company keep me?" If you can't come up with a good answer, maybe you should do something about it.

Ask yourself honestly whether you could do your boss's job better. If the answer is no, how do you change it to a yes?

Cut out the business jargon and say everything simply enough for a bright kid to understand. Clarity is worth a lot and jargon isn't worth a damn.

*Don't get married to the company. It might seem like a great idea, but companies are seldom faithful.*

Whenever it is important, make sure you have memorized all the facts. In arguments, the victory usually goes to the one who knows what they're talking about.

*When you win, make a point of being magnanimous. You may not win every time.*

*Learn to keep your temper in all circumstances. There is nothing so irritating as someone who can't be provoked into a row.*

*Even if you are not due to retire for many years, try writing your retirement speech. Imagine what you would say about your career while you still have time to make changes.*

Make a list of everyone who has moved or inspired you. Resolve to be more like those people.

*activities*
*and hobbies*

If it's years since you rode a bike, make a point of trying it again. It's even more fun now you're older.

Pick something you've never been able to do, like swimming, for example, and learn to do it. You'll be so proud of yourself for having overcome your inability.

*Set yourself a physical challenge: walk the Appalachian Trail from Maine to Georgia.*

*In-line skates—if you get the hang of them, think how impressed everyone will be!*

*Make a list of five books
you've always intended to
read but never got around
to. Give yourself a certain
amount of time to get through
each one.*

*If you can swim but not dive, then why not sign up
for a diving course? How hard can it be?*

*Buy a helium balloon, inhale
the gas—which is harmless—
and record yourself talking like
Donald Duck.*

Get a friend to take you to some place out in the
country and leave you there with a compass and a
map. It will test you both physically and mentally.

*If you don't have one, set up a nesting box in the garden. Watching your bird family grow up will keep you amused for hours.*

*Buy a yo-yo and try to remember how to do all those tricks you could do as a kid.*

Wait until everybody is out of the house and then put on your favorite CD and sing along while playing "air guitar."

You just have to try bungee jumping at least once. You'll never be quite the same again.

Learn to play bridge. It's sociable, competitive, and requires brains rather than luck.

Try to get an entry in the Guinness Book of World Records. *There's a huge range of challenges to choose from. You must be able to be best in the world at something.*

*Go to a winery and sample the wines. Many of them offer free tasting. Do this whenever you are in wine country.*

*Go to Egypt and visit the sights. Take the opportunity to ride a camel. It will probably be the worst riding experience you'll ever have but it's fun to say you've done it.*

Try jogging for twenty minutes morning and evening. It's not that enjoyable but if you stick with it, the health benefits are huge.

Why not take a course in first aid? You never know when you're going to need it.

*Become a blood donor. It's not every day you get the chance to save someone's life.*

*Even if you're not a Christian, try to read the Bible from cover to cover. It's full of interesting stuff that most people never read.*

*Take a vacation as a fruit-picker in the sunniest place you can find. The hard physical work will relax you mentally, and you'll meet lots of interesting people.*

# Take up pottery. It's creative, fun, and challenging.

*It's probably many years since you climbed a tree. Could you still do it? Try—but be careful!*

Swimming with dolphins has become a bit of a cliché but if you haven't done it, you should certainly give it a try.

*Watch a big sporting event with your partner but, just for once, skip saying, "What's all the fuss about?"*

Make a list of all those irritating jobs you should have done around the house but never quite got around to. Make a resolution to do at least one of them each week until they are all finished.

*In midsummer, why not try going for a night walk where you end up greeting the morning sun?*

*Track down a long-lost friend
and talk over old times.*

Be extra nice to the most irritating person you know. Maybe your change of attitude will be reciprocated.

*Give up using bad language
even when severely provoked.
You'll find that if you stop
swearing, you feel much calmer.*

Visit the beach in the middle of winter.
The crowds will have gone and you can
enjoy peace, quiet, and some brisk weather.

If you don't cook, take a beginner's course. Cooking isn't difficult, it's creative and, best of all, you can share the results with family and friends.

*Learn to paint in oils. Even if you think you're no good at painting, there is something about messing around with oil paints that brings out the creativity in the most unlikely people.*

Try glass blowing. It's not easy but it's a lot of fun and the end results often look interesting even if they're not quite what you intended.

*Try "googling" on the Internet. Using the Google search engine, you must construct a query that generates only a single response. It's harder than it sounds.*

*Take part in a Japanese tea ceremony. You don't have to go to Japan because there are plenty of places in the West where the ceremony is performed. It cultivates a very peaceful feeling in all the participants.*

It's probably a long time since you built a snowman, so why not do it again? If you feel embarrassed, get some help from a few children in the family and pretend that you're doing it for their amusement.

Have a snowball fight with your family and friends.

*Find a swimming pool with a really enormous slide and have a good time sliding down it.*

Learn to juggle. It is very good for relieving stress.

Make paper airplanes. You can find instructions for some really advanced ones if you search the Internet. If people laugh, explain that you have a serious interest in aerodynamics.

*Go and pick mulberries at the end of the summer and make a delicious pie.*

Try eating Scottish haggis! Love it or hate it, one thing is for sure—it'll be an experience you'll never forget.

*Take up the bagpipes or a French horn and thrill your neighbors with wonderful sounds.*

*Dig a pond in your backyard and stock it with goldfish. They are much more interesting than people think and there is something very calming about sitting and watching them swim.*

Spend a little time each day doing gentle bending and stretching exercises. It's good to stay supple as you get older.

*Decide to reorganize your home by throwing out all the junk you have accumulated over the years. Pretend you're going to move and see what you really want to take with you.*

Turn off the TV and talk to your family for a change. The art of conversation isn't dead, it's only unconscious. If you revive it, you will gain some real benefits.

*Are computers, e-mail, and the Internet a mystery to you? If so, take a course and learn about them. It isn't hard and there is a whole new world out there that you can explore.*

Give some of your time to charity work. It's great to give money but even better to give a bit of yourself.

*Get up early and go mushroom picking. Before you do this, be certain that you know which ones are safe to eat!*

*Tell your family that you're taking them somewhere really dull and then surprise them by taking them out for a meal instead.*

Baffled by the weather reports? Beat the weatherman at his own game and try to predict the day's weather first thing thing in the morning.

*Look at a map and plan a day trip to somewhere you have never been before.*

*Everybody should take at least one trip in a helicopter, glider, or hot-air balloon. If you're feeling wealthy, you could try all three.*

Celebrate Hogmanay (New Year's Eve) in Scotland. The street parties in Edinburgh and Glasgow are wild.

*Visit a local brewery if you can't get to the Carlsberg brewery in Copenhagen, Denmark or the Coors brewery in Colorado. Watching the brewing process is not all that interesting but they let you drink huge amounts of free beer when the tour is finished.*

Buy a breadmaker and bake your own bread. It's tasty, nutritious, and you don't have to worry about all the salt and additives that they put in the commercially made stuff.

In the summer, when soft fruit is plentiful, make your own preserves. It isn't much trouble to do and they taste ten times better than the ones you buy.

If you ever find yourself in Australia, why not walk right over the top of the Sydney Harbor Bridge? You wear a safety harness but, even so, it's wonderfully scary.

*Have you always wanted to write a book? If so, make this the year that you finally set pen to paper. Decide that this time you really are going to do it.*

*Pick some favorite poems and learn them by heart. As you get older, the memory becomes a little less reliable unless you take the trouble to train it.*

*Run a marathon for charity. It's not easy but all sorts of unlikely people have managed to do it. Start with short runs and gradually build up strength and stamina. It will be an achievement you always remember.*

How about being a space tourist? As time goes by there will be more and more chances for civilians to join a space mission. What's a few million dollars in comparison to the thrill of seeing the earth from space?

*Brew your own ginger beer. It's spicy, delicious, and because it has no alcohol, the whole family can enjoy it.*

Scan all your favorite family photos and save them on CD-ROM so that they can be enjoyed by generations to come.

*Buy a Chinese wok. It's the most versatile cooking utensil in the world and nobody who's serious about cooking should be without one.*

*Learning to ski combines excitement, exercise, fresh air, and après-ski enjoyment. Isn't it about time you took some lessons?*

Try building a ship in a bottle. It's not that hard when you know the trick (you can find the instructions on the Internet).

Join the texting revolution. It's fun, useful, and cheap.

*Find a four-leaf clover.*

Sponsor a Third World orphan.
Give someone a chance in life.

*Visit a chocolate factory. It may*
*destroy your taste for chocolate, which*
*will do a lot to help your waistline.*

*Have a limbo dancing party*
*while you're still supple*
*enough to get under that bar.*

*Try to get a good look at a tornado (from a safe distance).*

*Write poetry. You don't have to show it to anyone, but you might enjoy the creative process.*

Teach yourself to cook the perfect soufflé. It isn't nearly as hard as it sounds, but all your friends will be terribly impressed.

Build a model airplane. You can always pretend you're doing it to amuse a child—you!

Leave space in your backyard for wild flowers and butterflies. They're getting killed off by modern farming methods and need all the help they can get.

*Blindfold yourself and spend some time finding out what it is like to be blind. Only do this where you can't come to any harm.*

*Learn sign language so that you can talk to deaf people.*

*Try dowsing (you can find instructions on the Internet). It's an amazing experience when the dowsing rods go crazy in your hands.*

Find a neglected piece of land and
reclaim it for a community project.
Get your friends and neighbors to help.

Try a glass of Greek retsina. It's flavored
with pine resin and is very much an
acquired taste. The upside is that it
never leaves you with a hangover.

*Put all your small change in a jar
and once a year give the money to
the charity of your choice. You'll
be amazed at how all those nickels
and dimes add up.*

*At least once a week, make a point of having a meal
where the whole family sits around the table together.*

Go and join the studio
audience when your favorite
TV show is being made.

Do a sponsored
walk for charity.
Just remember to do
your stretches first.

*Spend some time just messing about
in boats. There is something
therapeutic about water and boats.*

Learn how to keep bees and produce your own honey. The life of bees is fascinating, and the honey tastes good too.

Learn to throw a boomerang so that it comes back to you. It's much harder than it looks.

Wait for a crisp winter's evening and take your whole family up a hill well outside town to view the stars.

Try eating frogs' legs. They are a bit like chicken but much nicer.

Go and visit the place of your birth.

Think ahead: make a will ensuring that your family and close friends—not the IRS—inherit your assets. Leave everyone a surprising present to remember you by.

*Learn to meditate. It will make you more serene and improve your health.*

Make a time capsule. Spend time with your family deciding what to include, then package it securely and bury it for someone to dig up in the future.

Try to spend some time living by the sea.

*Put the names of old friends into an Internet search engine and see how many of them you can find.*

Learn Esperanto, the man-made international language. It's easy and you'll get to talk to all sorts of interesting people.

*Make your own hovercraft. It's not hard (instructions are on the Internet) and it will keep you challenged and amused for months.*

*Make a return visit to your old school. See if you can find your initials carved on a desk.*

Visit a crop circle and see if you can figure out how it was done.

*Make a point of recycling stuff. Do your bit to save the planet.*

*However busy you are, set aside some time every day to talk to those closest to you.*

Plant a tree with someone you love. It will always be a special tree for you.

Learn to play the didgeridoo. Getting the circular breathing right will take you quite a while.

*See a whale or a great white shark in the wild.*

*Think of something you have always wanted to say to someone you know but have never had the courage to do so. Say it!*

Arrange a hot-air balloon flight for the whole family but don't tell them until just before they are due to go.

# nurturing the
## outer you

# Try a proper Swedish sauna.

*Eat a meal that includes real truffles. They're expensive but delicious.*

Lose some weight. Almost everyone would look better if they were a few pounds lighter.

*Make a radical change to your hair color. You might really like it and you'll never have to regret not having tried.*

Try eating snails in garlic butter. They're an acquired taste, but worth a try.

Fast for one day a week and give the money saved to your favorite charity. Your health will benefit and you can help a good cause.

*Get a henna tattoo. You can have all the fun of body art plus the security of knowing that it will come off in a couple of weeks.*

Give up alcohol for a week and see how much better you feel. Repeat from time to time for maximum benefit.

*Have an outfit tailor-made for you. We are all so used to off-the-rack clothes that we forget the sheer luxury of having something made.*

*Have a complete makeover from a qualified beautician. It will be expensive, but in future you'll know what makes you look good.*

Buy a pair of handmade shoes. It will cost a lot but they'll fit like gloves and you'll treasure them for years to come.

Have a Jacuzzi installed in your home. If you can't quite afford it, at least try one in a health club.

Go to the gym and get those muscles toned. You'll look better and your self-esteem will get a big boost.

*If there's something about your physical appearance that you've always been unhappy with, consider getting it fixed— cosmetic surgery needn't be drastic.*

Have your teeth capped and whitened. It costs a fortune, but it makes you look so much better.

*Now that you're fifty, have a complete medical checkup even if you don't think there is anything wrong with you.*

Put up a hammock in your garden. Sleeping in one takes a bit of getting used to (and you might fall out once or twice) but once you get the hang of it, you'll love it.

Get a sunless suntan. It's much safer than a real tan and it's said that Madonna and Britney use it, so who are you to argue?

*Drink a couple of small glasses of red wine each day (but miss out two days each week). A little red wine is good for your health.*

*Walking at least ten thousand paces each day will help you stay fit. It sounds like a lot, but you'll discover that it's nowhere near as difficult as you think.*

*Have a manicure to get those neglected nails looking glamorous.*

*A face pack will help freshen up tired skin and shrink those pores. These days, there are plenty of tempting varieties to choose from.*

*Have an aromatherapy consultation. You can benefit enormously from those relaxing vapors.*

Use acupuncture to help you give up a bad habit. It's said to be particularly good for quitting smoking.

*Take a course of self-hypnosis. It is easy to learn and can help to boost your confidence and eliminate negative thought patterns.*

Are you depressed? If so, you are not alone because 38 million Americans are suffering from depression.
Try Cognitive Behavior Therapy (sometimes called "the talking cure"). It has an impressive success record.

Many people find that the Alexander Technique has helped them to understand much more about how the body works, and how to make it work for them. Why not give it a try?

Change your shampoo.
For some reason no one
quite understands, a new
shampoo often produces
excellent results.

*Book a consultation with a perfume specialist.
She will tell you which scents smell best on you
and, if you are willing to pay the price, she'll help
you mix your very own personal perfume.*

Do eye exercises. You can
find the instructions on the
Internet. If you do them
regularly, they can reduce
your need for glasses.

*Exercise while sitting at your desk. A little gentle bending and stretching every so often will help to avoid common perils of office life such as backache and repetitive strain injury.*

When you have tired, aching muscles, give them a treat by rubbing brand wein into them. It has a delicious scent of pine and perks up a tired body. You get it from health food stores.

If you suffer from backache or other muscular problems, buy a novasonic massager. It uses audible sound waves to help ease your pain.

Make a paste with oatmeal and some plain yogurt. Don't eat it! The idea is to use it as a cheap, natural, and very effective facial cleanser.

*All the minerals and salt in the Dead Sea ensure that a dip there will give you an excellent body scrub. If you can't afford the trip, you can buy the minerals and salt in jars.*

Are you suffering from a lack of freshness in the foot department? Try this: combine two tablespoons of spearmint leaves, four ounces of rubbing alcohol, a little water, and a few drops of peppermint oil. The resulting paste will keep your feet sweet.

*Choose a hat. In fact, choose several and use them to express different facets of your personality.*

Let me guess—you joined a gym but never went. Am I right? So now get a personal trainer and really get your body back into shape.

Next time you get sick, try homeopathy. OK, logic says it can't possibly work but, on the other hand, there are lots of well people walking around saying that it cured them. What have you got to lose?

Moisturize, moisturize, moisturize. As you get a bit older, your skin needs all the help you can give it.

*You are always the last person to realize you have bad breath. Lift your palm, hold it to your nose, and breathe out. If your breath stinks you need to clean your teeth better, floss regularly, use mouthwash, and buy a tongue scraper.*

*Have your feet checked out by a chiropodist. Have corns, calluses, and bunions removed. How can you be happy if your feet hurt?*

*Next time you have something
to celebrate, hold a toga party.
You'll soon understand why those
Romans had such a good time.*

Why not wear a sari? They are colorful, light, and very elegant. They make excellent evening wear at a formal party.

*Have you considered getting
something pierced? There are lots
of choices and, if you don't like
the result, the piercing will
disappear in next to no time.*

If you feel a bit lacking in the lips department,
you can have collagen injections to give you that
bee-stung look. But beware—it sometimes goes
wrong and you can end up looking like a fish.

You could give your eyes a whole new look with colored contact lenses. A friend from India chose to have piercing blue eyes which, as you can imagine, caused a sensation.

*A week in a German health spa would really perk you up. The only downside is that they make you drink water full of natural minerals—very healthy, but an acquired taste.*

Buy some cool shades. They will protect your eyes and give you that sexy, mysterious look.

Wearing the right glasses can make you look more serious and intellectual. You don't need glasses? OK, buy some with plain glass in them. The effect remains the same.

*Take a body language course and learn what people's non-verbal signals are all about.*

If you've never streaked at a major sporting event, maybe you should consider it. Indulge the exhibitionist in you!

*Buy a backscratcher and you will enjoy hours of pure bliss.*

*By your age, it's likely that those stomach muscles are getting a bit flabby. Why not spend some time toning them up?*

*Get yourself invited to a black tie dinner. You'll look ravishing in a formal dress and your partner will be dazzled.*

*Did you know that drinking carrot juice is supposed to improve your natural coloring and make you look healthier? Try it and see.*

*Here's something that will make you look younger. It's called microdermabrasion and is a type of facial that gently removes the dead surface layer of skin.*

If your eyesight is not as good as it was and you don't like messing about with glasses or contact lenses, you could always try laser surgery. It's expensive but it could improve your eyesight and save you trouble.

*Take a tip from grandma and put a sprig of lavender under your pillow. It's supposed to lull you to sleep.*

*A concoction made from comfrey leaf, slippery elm, goldenseal root, and chickweed is supposed to be good for all sorts of nasty conditions, from bedsores to gangrene. If you don't know a comfrey leaf from a daisy, don't worry, you can buy the stuff ready-made.*

If, in a moment of madness, you once got a tattoo, do not despair. There are several ways of getting rid of it (excision, dermabrasion, laser treatment, and salabrasion). It may have seemed a good idea when you were twenty, but you've probably grown tired of it by now.

Face painting shouldn't be just for kids. In fact, adults often find it interesting as well as fun. Try it at your next party and experiment with new identities.

*Have you ever actually hugged a tree? Has anyone? Why not try it, purely in the spirit of scientific inquiry of course?*

*Try an orgasmatron. It's a cap of copper wires that you use to massage your head. The effects are extremely pleasant!*

Beekeepers swear that the upside of frequent bee stings is immunity to rheumatism. Personally I'm not about to try it, but you might take a different view.

*Biofeedback machines make a certain sound when you are completely relaxed. Therefore they can be used to teach you to how to achieve a state of relaxation. They are cheap and simple to use, so try one out.*

*How about having a sculptor carve your likeness? Vanity? No, you owe it to posterity.*

In some Eastern cultures, letting your little fingernail grow is supposed to bring great good fortune. If you're really desperate for some luck, it might be worth a try.

*Invest in a reflexology session. This Chinese technique is supposed to cure a wide variety of ailments.*

*Take a course in herbal medicine. In future, every walk in the country will be full of interest and excitement as you track down vital ingredients.*

Buy a crystal and wear it around your neck at all times. A little research will tell you the New Age significance of crystals and where to buy them.

*Study the psychological significance of various colors and dress according to the effect you want to create.*

If it gets chilly where you live, treat yourself to a genuine astrakhan hat. They don't come cheap, but they're stylish and very warm.

*Yet another idea for those who like something a bit different—apply some bindi body jewels. They are stuck on and can be removed easily.*

*Have a family photo taken wearing clothes from another era. You can rent the clothes from historical costumiers.*

Bathing in donkey's milk is not only good for the skin but is supposed to improve your libido. A little Internet surfing will reveal places that sell it.

You can have endless fun playing with hair extensions and wigs. Change your look completely and see if it improves your life.

*If you feel a bit slouchy as you get older, you could try walking around the house with a book balanced on your head. It worked for great-grandma.*

If you would like a fur coat but can't bear the thought of killing an animal, you could get one made of llama fur. It uses only the combings from the animal's coat.

*Try wearing a uniform for a day and see what difference it makes to your self-image. But don't get arrested for imitating a cop.*

"Gurning" is an old word for pulling ugly faces. It can be fun as a competition or a way of expressing your frustrations when facing the bathroom mirror. It's also good for the facial muscles.

If you are a certain age, you'll remember these lyrics: "Do your ears flip-flop? Do your ears hang out? Can you waggle them about?" Maybe now is the time to check this out.

*Do you have a nice smile? Many people have a really lousy one because they rarely get to see themselves smiling. Smile in front of a mirror and see if you need to improve your technique.*

Make a video diary. When you view it later, you'll learn a lot of interesting things about how you look and behave.

*Always walk confidently and fairly fast, especially if you're in a strange neighborhood. Muggers and other nasties are less likely to bother someone who looks like they know what they're doing.*

*If you get the chance, try a few breaths of pure oxygen. It's wonderfully enlivening. But don't get used to it because in large quantities it's toxic.*

It is said that drinking three glasses daily of one to two teaspoons of organic apple cider vinegar and honey dissolved in distilled water will keep old age at bay. That must be worth a try.

*Make a recording of your voice and listen to it carefully. You'll probably hate it (most people do) but this is the ideal opportunity to change the way you speak and make a better impression on people.*

*If your workplace still insists on formal clothes all the time, try campaigning for a "casual Friday" when you can all come in clothes that you actually want to wear.*

Buy a sportier car and feel those years just slip from your shoulders. Yes, it's immature behavior, but at your age who cares?

*When talking to someone you want to impress, it's a good idea to copy their gestures. This indicates that you are on the same wavelength. But don't overdo it or they'll think you are making fun of them.*

Some people swear that carrying a lot of money in their wallet makes them feel strong and act confidently. Of course, this only works for the right sort of people—all the others get worried about being robbed.

# ambitions
## and goals

*Write your biography. It doesn't need to be published but it will be instructive for you and interesting for your descendants.*

Take a flight in a microlight. Terrifying but fun!

**Leave the car at home once a week and go to work by bike. You'll be fitter, it will save on fuel, and you'll help the environment.**

*Take up one really difficult game like chess, bridge, or Go. These will all help to keep your mental powers up to scratch as you get older.*

*Go on a demonstration. What you demonstrate about is up to you, but at least once in your life stand up and be counted.*

Learn to dance. It's fun and excellent exercise. There are many styles to choose from and it will keep you active even when you are old.

Edit your entire wardrobe and get rid of all those clothes you're never going to wear again. Give the good ones to charity and dump the rest. Then reward yourself with a new outfit that suits the way you are now.

*You've been on this earth and enjoyed its resources for half a century. Now give something back by doing your bit for the environment: replace all the lights in your house with long-lasting, low-energy bulbs.*

*Go scuba diving. It will give you a whole new perspective on life.*

Make your own candles in time for the Christmas holidays. You can find instructions on the Internet and buy the ingredients from a craft store. It will add a little touch of special magic to your holiday season.

Make a piece of furniture (even if it's only a bookcase). You'll get years of use from it and have the satisfaction that it was made with your own hands.

Landscape your backyard. I bet it's just the way it was when you bought the house, isn't it? Why not sit down and plan a whole new layout?

*Hold a masked ball! They used to be common in high society but have gone out of style. The anonymity of the masks allows people to live a little.*

*Get a letter published in a newspaper. Think of something that really gets you worked up and write about it to the press. For once, be determined to say what you think.*

Get your eyes tested! Most people only bother when they feel they can't see clearly enough, but you should make the effort even if you think your sight is OK. Some eye problems can sneak up on you without your noticing.

Make a kite and fly it on a windy day. Of course you're only doing it to amuse the kids. But kite-making can be quite addictive and once you've made a simple one that works, you can graduate to more complex designs.

*Think of one thing you have always regretted and find a way to straighten it out.*

*Make a pilgrimage and test your endurance. You don't have to be religious to join the hordes of believers who make their way annually to places such as Mecca and Lourdes. It's a unique experience that will allow you to take stock of your faith and re-evaluate your life.*

*Come up with one completely original idea. It can be anything at all as long as it is entirely your own and not just a variation of someone else's notion.*

Think of one person you really admire and then try to meet them. It might turn out to be a wonderful experience that you treasure for ever.

*Go on an archaeological dig. They always need amateur volunteers to do the hard part and you might learn something really interesting.*

*Get elected to office. It doesn't have to be anything as grand as President of the US, but will give you the satisfaction of being chosen for something.*

Find out what your ideal weight should be and make a real effort to get there. You'll be delighted with both your willpower and your trimmer figure.

Compile a family tree. As you get older, your origins become more interesting.

*Why not study for a degree?*
*You can do it by distance learning*
*and, as well as being interesting,*
*it will boost your job prospects.*

Try to understand Einstein's theory of relativity. It's a great way to liven up the small talk at boring parties.

*Learn a new word every day. A large vocabulary will help you speak and write with authority.*

*Set yourself goals for one, five, and ten years ahead. Try to reach them all.*

Make a point of overcoming the thing you fear most. Whether it's snakes, spiders, or flying, you will feel so good about yourself when you find that you're not afraid any more.

*Ask your family what your most annoying habit is and make a determined effort to stop doing it.*

*Now work your way through the family and get them to stop their annoying habits. How happy you will all be!*

*Spend a whole day saying nothing that is trivial, stupid, or designed just to break the silence. Try to speak only when there is something of worth to say.*

Do a sponsored parachute jump for charity. You'll have a fantastic experience, do some good, and overcome your fears.

*Visit one of the poorest countries in the world to see just how lucky you really are.*

*Reorganize your daily schedule and see how much time you waste. Try to put the free time to better use.*

Ask the President of the US a question. You can do it from this Web site: www.whitehouse.gov

*Organize a fun run (just a couple of miles) in your locality, where runners get sponsored for charity.*

If you like the look of snowboarding but don't have the confidence to do it, start with sandboarding. The technique is similar but the runs are shorter and when you fall off, you land in nice warm sand.

*On a clear winter's night see how many shooting stars you can spot.*

Adopt a stray dog or cat from your local animal shelter.

How about taking flying lessons and working for your pilot's license? It's not cheap, but think of the thrill of being able to go where you want.

*Try to get your golf handicap down to single figures, turn your tennis serves into faultless aces, or simply brush up on your table tennis—just pick your favorite sport and get proficient at it.*

Re-read your old copy of Stephen Hawking's *A Brief History of Time*, only this time, try to understand it.

*If you never solved Rubik's cube, try it again.*

Pick one thing you really don't like about yourself and change it.

Read Tolstoy's *War and Peace* all the way through.

Get a short story published
in a magazine.

Become a proud pet
breeder and enter your
pets in competitions.

*If you had just one day
left to live, what would
you do? OK, now make
sure that you do it.*

*Build a treehouse for the kids in your family.
Test it yourself to make sure it won't fall down.*

Organize a sunflower-growing competition for your kids and their friends. The tallest sunflower is the winner.

*Learn to eat with chopsticks. It really isn't all that hard.*

***Invent a labor-saving device and make your fortune (or at least save yourself from a boring chore).***

If you're game for a challenge, you could learn rock climbing. It's an excellent way to get fit and it requires courage, skill, and strength.

Have a competition with friends to see who remembers most of the words to Bob Dylan's "Subterranean Homesick Blues."

*Grow the biggest pumpkin in the neighborhood in time for Halloween.*

Go panning for gold. It's time-consuming, can be hard work, and it won't make you rich, but you may end up with a little nugget to mark the occasion.

*On the mystery trail. . .try to be the first person to get a clear photo of a Bigfoot (Sasquatch).*

*Appear on TV. Everyone is supposed to have 15 minutes of fame, so make sure you get your turn.*

Join an amateur theater group and act in a play. Take all your friends along to tell you how good you are. Take your kids along to tell you the truth.

*Stick to the speed limit for a whole week and see how much gas you save.*

Plant catnip in your garden and watch all the local cats go crazy (it will also stop them from using your flowerbeds as a bathroom).

Make your life easy and save time in the long run by arranging all your books and CDs in alphabetical order. You'll be able to find exactly what you're looking for straight away.

*Try to eat vegetarian at least a couple of times a week and see your energy levels improve.*

Track down all your old classmates and arrange a get-together.

*Finish those long-overdue repairs on the car, or that decorating job, without resorting to bad language.*

# Get a part as a movie extra.

Find someone who needs cheering up and send them an anonymous surprise. Let them know that someone cares.

*Organize a treasure hunt for your friends. Give them a list of clues and then lead them all around your local area for a couple of hours. Give a small prize to the winner.*

Hold a quiz evening in your local school. Charge everyone a small entry fee, buy a prize for the winning team, and give the rest to school funds.

*Get up an hour early and see how much more you can get done in a day. Try it for a week and you'll wonder how you managed before.*

Take a sheep-shearing vacation in Australia. First you have to learn to shear sheep (which is the hard part). But then you can travel around Australia and get paid for it.

Write a song. Who knows, you may have a hit on your hands.

Go down to your local gym and do some weight training. You'll discover muscles you never knew you had.

*If you're handy with tools you could build your own house. You'd save money and get enormous satisfaction.*

Buy a metal detector and hunt for buried treasure. You might not find any gold, but you're sure to discover something interesting.

Think of five things you need to do to improve your home and work your way right through the list.

*Learn waterskiing. It is very difficult
but the feeling when you can finally
do it is worth all the effort.*

Try for a perfect score in bowling.

# Spend the night in a haunted house.

Sing "My Way" in a karaoke bar.

# *Take line dancing lessons.*

 Crash a really smart party by telling the guy on the door that you're "a friend of Bill's."

## *Take a vehicle maintenance course and save on all those garage bills.*

Repaint the outside of your house yourself. Be careful on that ladder!

Do some good in your neighborhood: go out for an early morning walk and pick up any trash making the area look untidy.

*Invite someone who lives alone to join you at Thanksgiving or Christmas.*

*Cultivate your psychic powers. See if you can bend spoons using only the power of your mind.*

Write your own list of things you want to do now you're fifty.

*Build a castle of playing cards. See how high you can go before it collapses.*

Try to light a fire by rubbing two sticks together.

Read a complete Shakespeare play and all the explanatory notes so that you actually understand it.

Next time your partner asks you to perform some chore you hate, make a point of doing it right away without having to be nagged and without complaining.

*Pick one of the seven deadly sins and give it up. They are pride, envy, gluttony, lust, anger, greed, and sloth, in case you'd forgotten.*

Decide to cultivate one or more of the seven contrary virtues. They are humility, kindness, abstinence, chastity, patience, liberality, and diligence.

*When you have succeeded with the sins and virtues, you could switch your attention to the seven corporal works of mercy. They are: feed the hungry, give drink to the thirsty, give shelter to strangers, clothe the naked, visit the sick, minister to prisoners, and bury the dead. See how many of these you can accomplish.*

Take a hot-air balloon flight and get an aerial photo of the place where you live.

Decide how you would like other people to think of you. Now try to live up to that description.

Work on a cure for the common cold.

*Find something useful to do with wire coat hangers and used teabags.*

Now that you're fifty, give up your job and start a completely new career that will revive all that enthusiasm you used to have.

*If you're married, hold a ceremony to renew your marriage vows.*

*friends*
*and family*

# Organize a surprise weekend break for your family.

*Think of the household chore your partner hates most and do it yourself.*

Bring your partner breakfast in bed.

## Organize a surprise birthday party for a friend.

When it's your turn to cook, tell the family that you are preparing something boring and then surprise them with a special meal.

Don't just assume that your family knows you love them, make sure you tell them from time to time (but not so frequently that it just becomes another habit).

*If you want a loyal friend who never tells anyone your secrets, buy a dog.*

*When you choose presents for your friends, make sure you give them what they want, not what they need.*

*Take the time to make those closest
to you feel they are beautiful.*

*The greatest gift you can give to
your children is independence
and the wisdom to use it.*

Listen carefully to those close to you.
You don't necessarily have to say
anything—often the listening is enough.

*Understand that just because you like all your
friends, they will not necessarily like each other.*

Include a "joke of the day" note in each of your kids' lunchboxes.

Get in the tub with your loved one and share a steamy bath together.

On Valentine's Day, send your partner a card in an envelope disguised to look like a bill.

Never let the goodbye kiss in the morning, or the coming home one in the evening, become habitual. Always kiss like you really mean it.

Do things together. It doesn't matter which things, it can even be paying bills or filling in your tax form, but it is always good to share.

*Write love notes on the bathroom mirror with the tip of your finger. When your partner gets out of the shower a note will appear in the condensation on the mirror.*

Quality time with your family doesn't mean watching TV together. Make sure you do interesting stuff regularly.

*Instead of everyone grazing from the fridge, make a point of getting the whole family around the table to eat together.*

*Phone from the office and leave a loving message on the voicemail so your partner will pick it up on returning home.*

*If you have young kids, have random tickle parties. Someone yells, "Tickle party!" and everyone tickles as many people as they can.*

If you can do anything unusual (e.g., juggle, ride a unicycle, or make owl noises by blowing into your hands) teach your kids how to do it.

Take an evening class with a friend. Learning is more fun if you share it (but don't get too competitive).

*If you can't use in-line skates, get your kids to teach you. You'll enjoy it after the bruises have worn off.*

*Hold a dance party with your kids. No one is allowed to sit out no matter how badly they dance.*

Get the kids to help you in the garden. If you can get them to be enthusiastic about growing things now, they'll thank you later.

Organize a treasure hunt with clues all around your neighborhood and a small prize for the winners. Kids will enjoy this long after they are "too old" for it.

*Have an impromptu concert. Use simple instruments like kazoos, harmonicas, and empty cookie tins for percussion.*

Get your whole family to sing and dance in the rain. It didn't do Gene Kelly any harm.

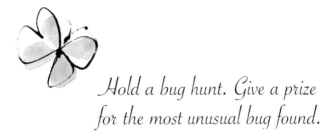

*Hold a bug hunt. Give a prize for the most unusual bug found.*

At a family gathering, suggest that everyone joins in singing "Kumbaya." Keep a straight face and don't forget to duck when they throw things.

*Dig out that fondue set that's hiding in the back of your closet and invite all your friends to a fondue party.*

*Take a midwinter dip with your friends. Last one to jump in is a sissy.*

Wear odd socks and wait for someone to remark on them. Then say, "Strangely enough I have another pair exactly like them at home!"

Take the whole family out for a picnic.

At New Year, go "first footing" like the Scots. You need to be dark-haired and carry a lump of coal and a bottle of whisky. If you're the first person to step over a friend's doorstep in the New Year, you bring them luck.

*Cook your family pancakes for no particular reason.*

*Persuade the children to cook and do the dishes on Mother's Day and/or Father's Day.*

*Make a collage of some of your favorite family photos and give it to your parents as a gift.*

Hold a seance. Try to get in touch with a departed relative or friend.

See who can make the best anagrams from the names of family and friends.

Pessimistic or wise? Plan an escape route in case the house catches fire. If the worst does happen, you'll have no time to wonder, "How do we get out of here?"

Make an effort to get along with a relative you have never liked. Invite them to dinner and try to heal old wounds.

*Watch TV with the sound down. Take turns to make up the silliest dialogue you can imagine.*

# Carve a Halloween pumpkin.

Go paintballing with friends and watch the gentlest of people turn into crazy, competitive loonies.

*Have a competition to see who can find the most original ways to spend $1,000,000. (You don't actually have to part with the cash.)*

*Give each member of the family an imaginary $10,000 to invest. Keep track of your investments and see who has made most money in six months.*

Ask all the family to state what their goal in life is. Write them all down and review them five years later.

Get the whole family to attack one really dreary household chore (stripping wallpaper, for example). When it's done, go out and celebrate.

*Go to a swimming pool with the largest slide you can find. Get all family members to go down the slide together.*

*Play a family game of Twister. If your family isn't big enough to make it interesting, you can invite a few friends over.*

Spend a family weekend camping.

*In hot weather, have a water fight.*

Have a family fitness campaign. Encourage each other to lose weight and do some exercise.

# *Buy a tandem bike with your partner and get fit cycling together.*

 Start a local fun run (say, two miles). Charge an entry fee to be donated to heart research. Give a badge to everyone who completes the course.

*Go to the kids' playground when there's no one around and have a go on all the equipment.*

Take turns to cook something completely new and experimental. The family gets to score each dish from one to ten.

*Have a movable feast with a group of friends. Go for drinks at one place, then appetizers at another, the main course at another and, of course, dessert at the last.*

# *Play bobbing for apples at a family party.*

*Tell your kids a funny story you have never told them before.*

Have your kids tell you something they did that no one found out about—it doesn't have to be something they'd be disciplined for!

*Start a book group with a small circle of friends. Meet regularly at different people's homes to discuss a book and drink some wine!*

*Take turns among friends to relate your most embarrassing experience.*

*Take turns with your family to relate your happiest memory.*

Share a book with a loved one by taking turns to read it to each other.

# Share a favorite poem with other family members.

Get one of those dance mats you hook up to the TV. Parents may look silly, but it helps everyone stay fit.

*Make a family video or audio tape and send it to a friend abroad.*

*Have a yard sale. Make some money out of all that junk and put it toward a fun family outing.*

# Work with your kids to dig a pond and stock it with fish.

Do crossword puzzles with your partner and expand your vocabulary.

*Have a Scrabble tournament in your workplace during your lunch break and find the office champion.*

**With your partner, carve your names somewhere really conspicuous.**

At the full moon, offer a small reward
for the first person who can spot the
rabbit in the moon. There is one, and
once you've found it you'll wonder
why you never saw it before.

Celebrate the end of
an enormous task.

*Take your partner on
a second honeymoon.*

*Throw a salsa party. Eat salsa, play salsa music, and dance salsa.*

*Pick out a cookbook, open it at random, and make whatever is described on that page.*

When at the beach, have a family sandcastle competition.

*Bury a family member up to the neck in sand.*

Have a family volleyball contest.

Play a family game of croquet. Beware—feelings run very high in croquet!

*Go beachcombing for unusual shells, driftwood, and cool rocks.*

*Take a banana boat ride. Laugh at anyone who slips off the banana.*

*Volunteer to read the map on a family journey. Keep your temper in spite of unfair criticism from the driver.*

*When abroad, master at least one nonsensical phrase in the local language. ("My nose is undercooked," for example.) Use it whenever possible.*

Walk barefoot in the park with your partner.

*Discuss your dreams with your friends. If you have any similar dreams, figure out what they could signify.*

*Start a family argument about whether it is correct to say "duck tape" or "duct tape."*

Find the most ridiculous things you can sell and buy on Ebay.

Build a Web site about you and your family. Post news and photos on the Web site so that far-off relatives and friends can keep in touch

*Take a pony-trekking vacation with the family.*

For the ultimate thrill, why not try skydiving? You and your partner can do it together and hold hands until it's time to release the chutes.

*Go to Chinatown and celebrate Chinese New Year.*

*Go green for St Patrick's Day! You don't have to be Irish (though it helps) but you must wear as much green as you can.*

Make a scary home movie in the style of *The Blair Witch Project*.

If the last time you went to a rock concert you had flowers in your hair, maybe it's time you went again. Take a group of old friends and pretend you're seventeen again.

## *Find the best firework display in your area.*

Take the family to the next open day at the fire station. Dare everyone to slide down the pole.

*Take the kids to your nearest theme park. See how many white knuckle rides you dare to go on.*

Go to a city or town council meeting and see just what the people who run your neighborhood are doing.

 Go to an auction and see what bargains you can get. Alternatively, sell something by auction and have fun watching the bidding.

*Make a point of holding doors open for people.*

Bake something for new neighbors to welcome them.

*Give a friend an unexpected compliment. Then do the same for a complete stranger.*

*Get everyone in the family to write down all the good things that have ever happened to them.*

*Give your family pet a birthday party.*

*Smile and wave at people in other cars. See how many return your greeting.*

love and romance

*You're never too old to send your lover a Valentine. Do it every year.*

Make your partner laugh out loud at least once each day.

Remember to say, "You look really great in that." Compliments are always welcome but we often forget to give them.

*Sit and reminisce together about your happiest memories.*

*Buy your lover small gifts—
nothing expensive or you'll look
guilty—for no reason at all.*

*Enjoy oysters and a glass of champagne together.*

*Spend a little time apart now
and then. It's so nice when
you get together again.*

Look through your old photos and remind
yourselves of what drew you together.

*When it's your anniversary, don't go to a fancy restaurant. Take the trouble to cook something special.*

*After a quarrel, always spend time making up before you go to bed.*

Say, "I'm sorry" when you know it was your fault.

Don't make a big thing of it when your partner is at fault.

Have a family hug now and then.

*Sing together, even if
you have lousy voices.*

Try to like, or at least tolerate, each other's taste in music.

*Write each other love
letters. You can say so
much more in a letter.*

*Spend a little time counting all the good qualities your lover has brought into your life.*

Take time to calmly discuss the things that cause you to quarrel.

*Oliver Cromwell said: "I beseech you, in the bowels of Christ, think it possible you may be mistaken." Pause to consider whether you might be at fault whenever you fall out with those you love.*

*Escape from the kids occasionally and enjoy a little quality time together.*

*When the kids finally leave home, you need to take time to rediscover each other.*

Tell each other funny stories from your past.

*Phone each other at work sometimes. Just a few kind words will be enough to make your day brighter.*

Make time to meet each other for lunch sometime during the working week.

*Remember that nagging is often just the repetition of unpalatable truths. Why not do as you're asked? You know it's for your own good.*

Keep a photo of your lover with you at all times.

Buy your partner tickets for a big sports match. He'll be stunned and he'll owe you a big favor in return.

*Make a special effort to get along with your partner's best friend.*

Agree that you are both
too old to be having the
mother-in-law argument.

*Form a united front when dealing with the kids
and refuse to let them play "divide and conquer."*

*Bite your tongue before
you say something hurtful.*

*Don't complain that your partner only
takes five minutes to buy what he wants
and he always gets a sale price.*

*Spend time planning your next vacation together. Sharing the planning can be almost as much fun as the trip itself.*

*Finish Do-It-Yourself projects that you start. Few things are less romantic than a gaping hole in the wall.*

Don't spend all your time at home talking about household stuff; make time to discuss things that you both enjoy.

Always share problems but don't let them take over your life.

Sleep in and have a
leisurely breakfast in bed
together from time to time.

*Sharing those irritating chores (like tidying
the garage) can turn a dull experience into
a feeling of shared achievement.*

*Wherever you keep your junk
(attic, basement, or lumber room),
spend some time sorting it together.
It's certain that happy memories
are lurking somewhere in the junk.*

*Learn something together. It doesn't matter whether it's a language or astrophysics, as long as you both enjoy it.*

Why not revisit places that hold special memories for you?

*Get rid of the TV in the bedroom. Surely you can remember when you had better things to do than watch TV in bed?*

Take lessons in map reading. How much domestic bliss has been shattered by people who can't read a map?

*When your partner says something, try listening. It's hard, but you can do it if you practice.*

Write a song for your lover. Sing it—even if you don't have a great voice it will be appreciated.

Do something really challenging together. Climb Everest? Explore the Amazon? The choice is up to you. All that matters is that you share a real adventure.

*Give each other a relaxing massage at the end of a long day.*

*If he snores, pack him off to the doctor to get it fixed. There is nothing more off-putting than sharing a bed with a snorer.*

Make a schedule for unpopular chores and stick to it. Nothing is less romantic than an argument about who takes out the trash.

Make a special effort to rediscover the magic in your relationship before the kids leave home.

*Admire and praise your partner's good points. With a bit of encouragement, even more good points might emerge.*

Write down the things you always argue about and make a pact not to mention them again.

*Take one of the kids' old cuddly toys and tuck it up in your partner's side of the bed. Yes, of course it's childish, but behaving immaturely can be quite romantic.*

*Do something on impulse. It can be anything you both enjoy but the important thing is that you decide on the spur of the moment.*

Have a professional family portrait photo taken.

*Turn off the TV and play games together. It can be anything from chess to Monopoly—the important thing is to enjoy it.*

*Rent a romantic video and watch it together.*

Camp out under the stars.

Organize a surprise party for your partner's birthday.

Wander hand in hand along
a deserted beach at sunset.

*Whisper sweet nothings like you
used to do when you were younger.*

*Choose a favorite song
to be "our tune."*

*Get a puppy or kitten to lavish affection on
when the kids are too old for that sort of thing.*

Why not go on a joint diet and try to look as slim and fit as you were when you met?

Hold hands! Why should only young lovers get to do this?

*Find the most impressive bit of scenery near you and go there to watch the sunset together.*

*Celebrate your silver wedding anniversary with an intimate candlelit dinner.*

*Invite all your friends to a really wild silver wedding anniversary party!*

*Go and help your grown-up kids decorate their new homes.*

Offer to look after your grandchildren so their parents can have much needed time off.

*Try to organize a family party where everyone has a good time and none of the relatives quarrel.*

Always be first to offer to make up after a quarrel. Never, never do the "We're not speaking" thing.

Give each other a hug from time to time just because you feel like it.

*Wait until your grown-up kids ask for advice—then give it unstintingly.*

Show an interest in each other's hobbies and pastimes. Don't switch off every time your partner talks about these things.

*Discuss interesting stuff you find in the newspaper.*

Buy some of that chocolate body paint. Use it with maximum imagination.

Leap out of bed, rush to the window, and yell, "Good morning, world!"

Make a real effort to be nice to your mother-in-law. You don't know how much longer she'll be around. Stop grinning!

*When shopping, split up and arrange to meet for coffee later. Men and women are psychologically incapable of enjoying a shared shopping experience.*

Do things that bring you into contact with younger people. You can be of help to them, and their energy and enthusiasm will help you to stay young.

*If you died today, what would you regret not having said to your partner? Say it!*

*Don't succumb to "grumpy old person syndrome." You're getting older but that doesn't mean you can't live with a smile on your face.*

Share money between you so that it doesn't cause quarrels. There's nothing like money problems to sour a relationship.

*If your partner is bad tempered, don't try to jolly them out of it. That never works. Just wait patiently for the mood to change.*

*Before finding fault with your partner, spend a few moments thinking about your own faults. Not so keen now, are you?*

*Spoil grandchildren but not so much that their parents get annoyed.*

If you have to argue, and we all do sometimes, do it in private. No one else wants to be involved.

*Loving your kids doesn't mean doing everything for them, it means helping them learn how to do things for themselves.*

A good row is sometimes beneficial. Like a thunderstorm, it clears the air. But always make up right away.

When your partner drives, make a point of looking out the window and not glancing nervously at the speedometer.

Anticipate the time when your kids will leave home and plan to help your partner through what might be a tough experience.

# Always talk, never yell.

*Tell each other plainly what you really want. Don't think that just because your partner can't read your mind, they don't care.*

*When a kind thought comes to you, say it out loud. When you think of a cutting remark, keep it to yourself.*

Realize that you won't be together for ever. Make the best use of your time.

*Take a walk together in freshly fallen snow and come home to a mug of hot chocolate.*

*Stop yourself from telling the same
anecdotes over and over again.*

When the vacation photos
arrive, grant each other the
right of veto over any that make
you look fat, old, or crazy. But
if you can bear it, consider
keeping hold of them for a
giggle ten years down the line.

*Resist telling friends
funny stories where your
partner is the fall guy.*

*Praise your partner's BBQ skills. Quietly trim off the burned bits without drawing attention to them.*

*Sing along to soppy love songs together.*

Call each other by the pet names you used to use years ago. Don't pretend you've forgotten—you're fooling nobody.

When you're having a good evening, resist saying, "Oh well, time for bed." Live a little!

*Always search for new things that inspire you both with enthusiasm.*

Go through this book with your partner and choose ten things that you'd both like to do very soon.

# exploring the
## inner you

*Learn to meditate. It's not hard to do, will relieve your stress symptoms, and help every area of your life.*

Count your blessings. It's easy to take the good things in your life for granted while you worry about the bad bits. So make sure that, every so often, you acknowledge all the best things in your life.

Decide to keep a diary and make sure you do it. You'll find it really helps you to resolve your problems and it will provide you with something interesting to read when you're older.

*Keep a dream diary and note down all the dreams you remember. Dreams can often be a source of creative inspiration.*

Have your handwriting
analyzed by a graphologist.
You may be saying more
than you think when you
write to people.

Have your birth chart drawn up by an astrologer.
No of course you don't believe in it—but few
people can resist having a look at their own chart.

*Make a self-improvement
list and see how many
items you can cross off in,
say, the next three years.*

Get your blood pressure tested. High BP often
has no symptoms but can do you serious damage.

*Learn to visualize the things you would like to happen. Making them real in your mind is an important step to making them real in the outside world.*

# Take a polygraph test. Can you outwit the lie detector?

Take a few minutes to review your day and decide what went well and what disappointed you. It's worth checking your progress so that life doesn't just slip by.

*If you have any special knowledge or skill, try teaching it in an evening class. It will increase your enjoyment and give others a chance to share your know-how.*

Take an ESP (extrasensory perception) test. Do you have psychic powers? You'll never know unless you do a test.

Take an IQ test. If you always suspected you were a genius, now's your chance to prove it.

Now try an EQ (emotional quotient) test. Make sure your emotions are all in good order.

Test your concentration. Take a simple picture and see how long you can hold it in your mind when you close your eyes. With practice, your concentration will strengthen.

Calculate your body mass index (instructions are to be found on the Internet). Maybe now you'll trim off a few of those extra pounds...

*Try a Lüscher color test. It analyzes your personality according to color preference.*

Find the numerological significance of your name. Instructions can be found on the Internet.

An endoscopy (where a tiny camera is passed down your throat) will certainly show the inner you. Not recommended just for fun but if you have to have one, it is very interesting for those who are not too squeamish.

*Go to assertiveness classes and see what a difference they make to the way you behave. You'll soon have an air of calm and authority that will boost your confidence.*

Go into psychotherapy. There doesn't have to be anything wrong with you, but it would be interesting to discover how your mind works.

*Discover your demons. What are you most afraid of? Once you know what they are, you can start to defeat them.*

*What things do you treasure most in life? Some are obvious, but if you write a list you may find things that surprise you.*

Find your core beliefs. These are the thoughts that lie at the very root of your personality and you can spot them because they will produce strong emotions every time you access them.

Do a heart stress test. Your doctor will get you to walk and then run up a sloping treadmill. If you have heart problems, this test should find them.

*Do breathing exercises. As you get older, your lung capacity decreases unless you do something about it.*

*Eat five portions of fruit and
vegetables each day. It will help
protect you against major killers
such as cancer and heart disease.*

*Drink at least two quarts of water
every day. It keeps you healthy
and makes you look younger.*

Take time to review memories
of your youth. With maturity,
you will understand things that
you missed the first time around.

*Draw a self-portrait. It doesn't matter if you are no artist—just making the attempt will give you valuable insights into your character.*

# Consider this—if you were an animal, which one would you be?

 Do this with friends: each write a list of five adjectives that best describe the other members of the group.

When you need inspiration, get your friends together and have a brainstorming session. You are allowed to say anything, even if it appears to make no sense at the time. Insights will eventually emerge.

A fairy gives you three wishes. Decide what you would wish for. Be careful! You've read enough fairy tales to know how dangerous this wish business can be.

Imagine you have been given a bottle containing the elixir of life. If you drink it, you'll be forever youthful. Decide whether or not to drink it.

Look at yourself in the mirror each morning and say, "In every day and every way, I keep getting better and better." In time you'll start to believe yourself and beneficial changes will occur.

Spend time visualizing the sort of life you would like to lead. The more detail you can include, the better. The visualization isn't magic but it will help you to achieve the life you desire.

*Tell someone important to you that you love them. Don't just leave them to guess at your feelings.*

Think carefully about someone you deeply dislike. Try to get to the root of your antipathy and see if there is anything you could do to make your feelings less hostile.

*Think of one thing you could do that you would like to be remembered for when your life is over.*

Spend time thinking of the characteristics you most dislike in others. Could it be that you are guilty of the same faults?

*Take the time to ponder on the qualities you most admire in others. How far could you go in emulating these good qualities?*

We all think about stuff that is not worth the time we devote to it. Think of the thing that wastes most of your time and make the effort to delete it from your thoughts.

We often put up with behavior from others that we find unacceptable but don't have the courage to criticize. Think of the one thing that bugs you the most and, taking your courage in both hands, politely ask the offender to stop.

*Remember the happiest day of your life so far. What does your choice tell you about yourself?*

*Do you put off jobs that bore you?*
*Yes, we all do it. But now try to do*
*every job just as soon as it arises.*
*You'll feel so much better and may*
*be able to make this a habit.*

## Select three quotations from famous people that you think have a special resonance in your life.

Invent a saying that you would like to be remembered for in the future.

*Draw up a complete list of all your strengths. Any sort of ability (physical, intellectual, emotional, or spiritual) can go on the list.*

*Now make a list of your weaknesses. Don't beat yourself up, just be as honest as possible.*

*Now consider what opportunities are open to you. What things could you achieve with a bit of effort?*

Now think of all the things in life that get in your way and stop you reaching your full potential. Slowly but surely, make sure you remove these obstacles.

*If you have the opportunity to work with kids or teenagers, do it. They will highlight your good and bad points without mercy. If you're tough enough to survive the experience, it will do you good.*

By the age of fifty, life will have dealt you a few blows. Make sure you always get up one more time than you get knocked down.

 *Always have one thing you are passionate about and feel that passion fuel the rest of your life.*

Make the effort to learn to focus. Your energy is more effective if you concentrate on one task at a time.

*Only a few people in life are really special to us. Make sure you keep a lookout for such people and don't let them slip by unnoticed.*

*Think of something that makes you*
*special and marks you out from the crowd.*
*Now work to develop that quality until*
*it lights up your whole life.*

Always think, "Who am I?" The answer is harder to find than it appears, but once you have it, your life will be transformed.

*Think of something you*
*would do if you knew you*
*could not fail. Now go*
*ahead and do it anyway.*

*Passion is automatic, but love is not. If you want to*
*love, you must make the effort to do so.*

*Refuse to accept limitations on your ability. Only when you accept them, do they become real.*

Take time to be creative. It doesn't matter what you create, it is the process that is important.

*The Chinese say that it isn't the mountains ahead that wear you out, it is the grain of sand in your shoe. As you get older, have the wisdom to remove that sand.*

*If you think you are too small to affect the world, take a moment to consider the butterfly that flaps its wings and causes a hurricane.*

*Renew yourself constantly. Make a new start every day. Don't ever let your life become "the same old thing."*

Have the courage to let go of what you are and become what you might be.

*What you say is less important than what you do. People will often forget what you said but will remember your deeds.*

Embrace your problems.
As each is solved, it will
strengthen you a little more.

*Grow! Mentally, physically, and spiritually, you must never cease to grow.*

*The most difficult but most valuable thing we can ever do is to recognize that we ought to control our thoughts.*

*The most important thing you will ever do in life is to give birth to yourself by becoming what you potentially are.*

The Chinese say, "The birds of worry and care fly above you and there is nothing you can do, but you can prevent them building nests in your hair."

*Nelson Mandela said, "A good head and a good heart are always a formidable combination." Try to cultivate both.*

*There are few emotions as warm, comforting, and seductive as self-pity. Make sure you always tear it out by the roots before it smothers you.*

What things do you do when you think no one is looking? This is the person you really are deep inside.

It is not just important to be yourself, you should also give those around you the space and the opportunity to do the same.

*Make a point of showing gratitude when it is due. It is one of the greatest virtues.*

Anyone can be busy. Even ants are busy. It is important to be busy with something that matters.

*Walk only the paths where you find obstacles blocking your way. The paths without obstacles lead nowhere.*

No one can teach you anything but if you are wise, you'll let them help you to find out for yourself.

*Keep your mind flexible.*
*Only rigid things break easily.*

Age gives you a
choice: you can let it
make you mellow or
you can let it rot you
through and through.

Climb a mountain and it is not the
mountain you conquer, but yourself.

*In the whole universe, the only place you can be sure of making an improvement is in your own mind.*

*Work at spreading light, either by becoming the candle or the mirror that reflects it.*

*Nice guys don't finish last. Nice guys win before the race even starts.*

Confucius said, "To see what is right and fail to do it is want of courage."

Don't be afraid
to play and be
frivolous. These
things wake up
the brain cells.

*Thought is good but you'll never plow a
field by turning it over in your mind.*

*Use your brains. Many people get
through life without doing this, but
the lives they live are poor things.*

*People are so intent on changing the world that they forget that the best way to do it is to change themselves.*

 As you grow older, you need to remember that it is never too late to become what you might have been.

The best way to polish your brain is to rub it vigorously against others.

# Blaming others robs you of the power to change.

Keep your eyes wide open for opportunity. Unless you are vigilant, it can slip by without your noticing.

*Once you let a new idea stretch your mind, it will never shrink back to its old shape.*

*Make a point of putting away anger. Every minute you are angry, you lose 60 seconds when you could have been happy.*

*Make sure you change
when you see the light and
not when you feel the heat.*

You don't get to choose how or when you will die.
But you can choose how to live. Do it now.

*If you are going to
walk on thin ice, you
might as well dance.*

If you want to understand yourself, you
need to take the time to listen to others.

*Make your actions speak for you and not your intentions. You may have a heart of gold, but then so does an egg.*

If you would bring about a new and better world, you must first create it in your mind.

*The past and the future are not accessible to you. The only place you can do anything worthwhile is right now.*

*You only live once but get your attitude right, and once will be enough.*

*What you will leave behind has*
*nothing to do with stone monuments*
*and everything to do with the minds*
*of those you touched.*

Even if life is not the party you
hoped for, remember that
anything can happen. A world
of opportunities may be waiting
just around the next corner.

*Don't take life too seriously.*
*No one ever gets out of here alive.*

*We haven't the faintest idea what life is really all about. The most you can do is live it to the best of your ability.*

Don't hide your troubles away, but share them with those close to you. How else will they show they love you?

Try to be brave. It helps to know that courage consists mainly of being the only one who realizes just how scared you are.

Leave nothing that is in your heart unsaid. No one will know unless you tell them.

*Give a rose and the fragrance of giving lingers on your hand.*

*Wise people know what they should do next. But only brave ones do it.*

*This book is dedicated to the memory of Robert. While he might not have completed everything on this list, he came closer than most. Here's to hoping this book might inspire others to follow suit. Never allow life to simply pass you by.*

MQ Publications Limited
12 The Ivories, 6–8 Northampton Street, London N1 2HY
Tel: +44 (0) 20 7359 2244  Fax: +44 (0) 20 7359 1616
email: mail@mqpublications.com
www.mqpublications.com

Copyright © 2005 MQ Publications Limited
Text © 2005 Robert Allen
Illustrations © 2005 Robyn Neild

ISBN: 1-84072-798-5

1 3 5 7 9 0 8 6 4 2

Printed and bound in China.